REALISMPHOTOREALISM

FRONT COVER
Alfred Leslie
Detail from SEVEN A.M. NEWS
Oil on canvas, 84 × 60 in.
Courtesy: Joseph Shein, Philadelphia, Pennsylvania

BACK COVER
James Valerio
Detail from GAIL
Oil on canvas, 84 × 72 in.
Courtesy: Stephen S. Alpert, Wayland, Massachusetts

This catalogue documents the exhibition REALISM/PHOTO-REALISM, organized by guest curator, John Arthur, for Philbrook Art Center, Tulsa, Oklahoma, and presented from October 5th through November 23rd, 1980. Publication of the catalogue was assisted by The Williams Companies of Tulsa. The exhibition was assisted by the Oklahoma Humanities Committee, the National Endowment for the Humanities (a federal agency), and The Williams Companies.

REALISMPHOTOREALISM

October 5 – November 23, 1980   Philbrook Art Center, Tulsa, Oklahoma

Essays, catalogue and selections by John Arthur

Realism/Photo-Realism represents another step in Philbrook Art Center's exploration of the art of the western tradition for the people of Tulsa and the Southwestern Region of the country. In a previous exhibition, Gloria dell'Arte, Renaissance realism and its use of perspective was studied. Major developments in the history of realism were then surveyed in A Century of French Masters: Corot to Braque. This exhibition draws attention to contemporary realism and its two major manifestations. It is the hope of the museum that the exhibition will continue to throw light on artists' efforts to deal with reality and to present their views of it to the public.

We wish to thank John Arthur, an Oklahoma native and a graduate of The University of Tulsa, who curated the exhibition. It represents his ability to assemble important pictures and provide insight into this movement.

Thanks to the artists, the galleries, museums, and private collectors for participating, and especially to Ralph Goings and Alfred Leslie for producing prints for the opening.

The exhibition is made possible by a generous grant from The Williams Companies of Tulsa, the Oklahoma Humanities Committee, and the National Endowment for the Humanities. We wish to thank, in particular, Joseph H. Williams, the Chairman of the Board of The Williams Companies, for his support of this program.

Further thanks go to Benjamin F. Boddie, Vice President, Corporate Communications for The Williams Companies; Graham Sudbury, Director, Public Relations; Michael R. Dixon, Director, Communications; and Douglas J. Butterworth, Graphics Designer, for their help in preparing this publication.

Jesse G. Wright, Jr.
President/Director
Philbrook Art Center

REALISM PHOTOREALISM

P hilbrook holds a special and unique position for me. Prior to my first visit during high school, I had only known works of art through reproductions and books. Walking through the Kress Collection I experienced for the first time that sensation of encountering another milieu and continent through the special vision of an artist, and the capacity of painting from another century to evoke a sense of *deja vu.* Unlike the study of history, those works gave their epoch a clarity and intimacy, and freed it from the tedium of facts. That reaction remains a vital part of my criteria in evaluating works of art.

It was also at Philbrook that I encountered Alexander Hogue's painting, *Mother Earth Laid Bare,* and in Tulsa the architecture of Bruce Goff. A few years later, both men played an extremely important role in shaping my ideas.

Like so many students before and after me, I taught classes in the museum's educational program, and close friends from college are now on the staff.

Jesse Wright has contributed heavily toward elevating the import of the museum to the city and its status in the museum world. I am grateful for the opportunity he has given me to curate this exhibition, and extend my thanks to Philbrook's highly supportive and professional staff.

To organize this exhibit is to report back home.

Without the assistance and cooperation of the painters, dealers, collectors and institutions organizing and securing loans for such an exhibit would be an impossible task. I extend to them my thanks and gratitude.

In the end, a curator is always frustrated with the exclusions, brought on by space restrictions and conflicts with other exhibits.

Chuck Close, Don Nice, Rackstraw Downes, Sidney Goodman, and Catherine Murphy, to name but a few, have contributed heavily to the shape of contemporary realism. To them, and to the viewers, I apologize for their absence.

John Arthur

inda Nochlin, the noted art historian, has described nineteenth century realism as a "truthful, objective and impartial representation of the real world, based on meticulous observation of contemporary life."[1] Her description also accurately characterizes the work in general of the contemporary Realists and Photo-Realists.

To their credit, these painters do not subscribe to a program. Not only are their works stylistically discernable from each other, but they could never be mistaken for their American and European nineteenth century counterparts.

It is a mistake to assume that such a high degree of verisimilitude reflects an "objective and impersonal" representation of a simpleminded accurate transcription of nature, particularly in regard to the Realists.

Jack Beal, Alfred Leslie, Alex Katz, and William Beckman (in spite of the meticulously informed appearance of his work) are, for example, clearly subjective and interpretive painters.

Perhaps much of what we label as "Realism" today would more accurately fit the description of "Naturalism," but the matters of polemics and esthetics I will gladly leave to other writers. For as Annie Dillard has observed, ". . . the question of the tale, teller, and world fades into the question of the relationship between any perceiver and any object."[2]

[1]Linda Nochlin, REALISM, Pelican Books, 1971
[2]Annie Dillard, IS ART ALL THERE IS?, Harpers, August, 1980

REALISM

It was a matter of my trying to find subjects that are generally discredited — subjects that have, perhaps, been treated falsely by a lot of other painters, subjects that were part and parcel of the literature of painting — to take them and try to find truth in those subjects. I think there are truths in old people, truths to be seen in babies, nursing mothers, children, and family life. I may not be the one who is able to do it, but I think that those subjects, inherently, are fine subjects. And if I can't do it, then I hope that some quality of the effort that I make can be passed on to someone else who may have a better way of looking at it, maybe with more skills, more analytical strengths to make convincing the values of everyday life, including family life.

Alfred Leslie, *Drawing,* **Vol. I, No. 4, Nov., Dec. 1979**

ike most upheavals in the arts and sciences, Abstract Expressionism opened many new avenues for exploration. Sensibilities as diverse as those of Jasper Johns, Robert Rauschenberg, Andy Warhol, Kenneth Noland, Larry Rivers, and Richard Diebenkorn, for example, clearly and intelligently reflect the influence of the Abstract Expressionists.

Abstract Expressionism was also the dominant force behind contemporary Realism. It is this connection that remains a major factor in separating "new" Realism from the earlier Realism of Edward Hopper, Charles Sheeler, and the American Scene painters and distinguishes them from other contemporary figurative artists such as Andrew Wyeth, Ben Shahn, and Leonard Baskin, who have refused to acknowledge the significance of Abstract Expressionism.

In fact, most of the first-generation, "new" Realists had direct contact with the Abstract Expressionists. There were warm and close relationships between them that often went beyond an exchange of ideas. Many of the Realists began their careers as abstract painters.

The influence of Abstract Expressionism on the Realists and Photo-Realists can be seen in their incorporation of the physicality of the paint (Fairfield Porter, Wayne Thiebaud, Neil Welliver, Jane Freilicher, for example), abstract and/or expressive use of color (Jack Beal, Lowell Nesbitt, Robert Cottingham, Janet Fish, Alex Katz), a more conceptual depiction of space and composition (Jack Beal, Alfred Leslie, Philip Pearlstein, Stephen Posen, Richard Estes, Robert Cottingham, and John Clem Clarke), and the large scale canvas (Alex Katz, Alfred Leslie, Lowell Nesbitt, Joseph Raffael, James Valerio, etc.) as opposed to easel painting.

Also characteristic is the harmonious juxtaposition of past and present influences, such as Fairfield Porter's acknowledged influence by de Kooning and Vuillard, Alfred Leslie's carry-over of Abstract Expressionist devices fused with the light of Joseph Wright of Derby, the narrative of Copley, or an update of a Cole scene, and Beal's radical composition wedded to Dutch themes and light.

It is significant that the exclusion of figurative elements was not a major factor in Abstract Expressionism; especially in the

work of Arshile Gorky, Jackson Pollock, and Willem de Kooning. In particular, such paintings as Pollock's *Portrait and a Dream* and de Kooning's *Women* had younger painters, such as Leslie, Rivers, and the de Nagy group, proclaiming the birth of a "new realism" in the early fifties.

Ironically, the most misunderstood fact in regard to contemporary Realism is the time of its development. It is not, in spite of many articles to the contrary, an occurrence of the seventies. The first generation of "new" Realists matured as artists during the same period as the post-Abstract Expressionist formalist painters. However, for the better part of a decade, much of the art establishment (the art schools, institutions, and critics) refused to consider these painters' presence as a serious and viable aspect of contemporary art.

The mature work produced by Realists such as Fairfield Porter, Wayne Thiebaud, Philip Pearlstein, Alfred Leslie, Jack Beal, Alex Katz, Jane Freilicher, and John Button now spans a period of twenty years, a fact that alone indicates that Realism is more than a minor diversion in contemporary art. The maturation of Realism parallels the coming of age of these painters, who, with the exception of Jack Beal, are now fifty or older.

By the beginning of the sixties, there was already Realist painting that was essentially the same as that which is so distinct and highly recognizable today. The basic difference is that the work from the early sixties looks more loose and painterly than current paintings by the same artists. Of course, in the context of Abstract Expressionism and color field painting, by comparison it looked tight.

Today the sharp division between the two major forms, Realism and Photo-Realism, hinges on painting based primarily on direct observation as opposed to painting derived from photographic source material.

Certainly not a minor feature of Realist and Photo-Realist painting is the matter of craft. It is particularly noteworthy in regard to these painters because they were educated in one of the rare periods when emphasis on the craft of painting, skills of direct observation, and traditional controls over the formal elements had almost atrophied to the point of being abandoned in art schools throughout the country. In order to make the paintings they have chosen to make, many Realist artists have had to teach themselves the necessary skills. With a developed control of the craft and the self-confidence that gaining those abilities entails, the end results have grown increasingly more impressive.

In the worst examples of Realism and Photo-Realism, the servant — craft — has become the mistress. The viewer is served high style and shallow content; and when image and content fail to blend harmoniously and intelligently with style and craft, there is a sad lack of probity and resonance.

The Abstract Expressionist-Realist link is most clearly exemplified by the painting careers of Fairfield Porter and Alfred Leslie. Fairfield Porter is to Realism as Jackson Pollock is to Abstract Expressionism. Porter's work was always held in high esteem by painters, and since his death in 1975, regard for his stature as a painter has grown considerably. But it is still underestimated.

In terms of his age, Porter was a peer of the Abstract Expressionists. He graduated from Harvard with a degree in art history and later studied painting at the Art Students League. Porter's criticism has been widely acknowledged for its independence and lucidity. He had that rare ability to approach a broad range of art not from a fixed esthetic position but on terms inherent in the work. His openness to a plurality of expressive means was evident in his writing, which covered more than three decades.

Porter's friendship with de Kooning developed in the late thirties. He was the first to write about de Kooning's work although ironically the piece was turned down by the *Partisan Review* and other periodicals on the grounds that de Kooning had not achieved the stature to merit such coverage.

Porter was also friendly at that time with the critic Clement Greenberg, though he adamantly opposed Greenberg's narrow esthetic doctrine, especially his insistence that figurative painting was no longer viable in contemporary art. According to Porter, Greenberg's hard-line esthetics dissuaded him from attempting abstraction as a painter.

Porter was not a natural, instinctive painter. His work was studied and deliberate. The look of spontaneity and ease belies the labor and calculation beneath the surface of his best work, and his composition is often stiff and awkward. The ability to be critically objective about his own painting, coupled with iron-willed determination and prodigious effort, underlies his most beautiful results. As with all memorable painters, we forgive and forget the failures and mediocre paintings and remember only the best efforts.

Porter had that uncanny ability to hold sight of a brief, flickering moment, ever so transient, and to retain its nuance through the sustained act of developing a painting. He could summarize that response and crystallize a specific experience in highly communicative visual terms. This ability, coupled with the power to distill to its essence a momentary mood through the process of painting, is at the core of his

strength as an artist.

Columbus Day, one of Porter's greatest paintings, is an image and an idea stripped to its essentials. Nothing detracts. No part is superfluous to the whole. Color, light, and sensation solidify in this brief moment in his back yard. It is the distillation of an emotional shiver authenticated by the painter's intellectual capabilities. This image, frozen in time and devoid of sentimentality or ingratiation, touches a nerve, and becomes the back yard of all America.

Alfred Leslie is the only Realist who achieved a major reputation as an Abstract Expressionist. To abandon a hard-won position and a sizable reputation in pursuit of an expressive mode held in low esteem in the art world would, one can only speculate, make the metamorphosis toward Realism an unlikely pursuit for an artist less strong-willed than Leslie.

In terms of content, the distance between Abstract Expressionism and Realism is not an impossible span. Abstract painting can signify emotion or imply an aspect of the tangible world. Seen this way, the difference between abstraction and Realism is a matter of emphasis.

A narrative edge has existed in Leslie's work from his early abstractions through the present. For example, stripes in several Abstract Expressionist paintings refer to an American flag on his studio wall, and fragments in the collages are litter from the floor and trash basket, ironic autobiographical shards. Leslie has also worked in associations with poets and writers and made forays into film such as *Pull My Daisy,* written and narrated by Jack Kerouac, and *The Last Clean Shirt,* a collaboration with Frank O'Hara.

As Leslie's energies became more focused in his paintings, the narrative impulse that had found expression in film, photography, and writing began to emerge in the form of more highly articulated and content-oriented images.

As a Realist, Leslie comes too close to truth for comfort. In his paintings he not only upholds the virtues and strengths of family life but also warns us of contemporary dangers. *7:00 A.M. News* depicts a solitary woman at a meager breakfast. Her only visible contact with the outside world is through the electronic device of the portable T.V. set, which broadcasts a tragic vignette of Third World politics, and the mechanically produced morning paper displaying two photographs of events of the previous day: an ominous hooded figure and a highlight from a basketball game. The three representations are presented with equal import and are numbly accepted without evaluation as indisputable and inevitable truths.

Even when the supply of Morris Louis and Friedel Dzubas paintings is exhausted, we will not see paintings like *7:00 A.M. News* in the lobbies of our banks and corporations, for they depict truths that evoke discomfort and elicit thought and self-examination.

Perhaps it was the experience of painting at night and working in the daytime as a draftsman for many years, combined with a preference for static, neutral light that articulates without suggestion of drama, that has led Philip Pearlstein to cover the windows of his studio with black paper and work under three fixed lights. He chooses a light that clearly articulates the minute details of the models' anatomy without suggestion or sensual inference, like the light over an operating table.

Since 1960 Pearlstein has painted nudes in the studio. His paintings of the figure are never glamorized. Because of the abrupt cropping, they are often depersonalized, even striking the viewer as being simply people with their clothes off rather than adhering to our preconceived notions about the nude derived from several centuries of painting and several decades of voyeurism via magazine depictions.

In the sixties it was easy to mistake Pearlstein's objectivity for academicism. As his paintings became increasingly descriptive of the physical facts of the flesh, he was often accused of working from photographs. Today he is often accused of being impersonal, as though that were a fault rather than part of his esthetic, and he is subjected to ridicule by academic painters steeped in the study of anatomy who are critical of his distorted proportions, an issue which has been null since Cezanne. The fact is, this distortion occurs as a result of the tight quarters in his studio. With such close proximity to the model, his painting is a bit like piecing together a panoramic photograph. There are no accidents in Pearlstein's work.

His composition and his use of planes and cropping are closer to the abstract constructions of painters such as Al Held than to traditional representational art. Opportunities for color, pattern, and complexity beyond the form of the figure are heightened by Pearlstein's use of rugs, Indian blankets, and antique furniture, which he makes us see as abstract structures first and functional objects second.

Pearlstein has brought a renewed viability to figurative painting and has made a major contribution to the redefinition of Realism in post-modern terms. Ironically, his equalized attention to all the visual data contained in a picture and his deadpan objectivity have more deeply affected the look of Photo-Realism than direct-observation Realism.

While Pearlstein has pushed the informational boundaries of visual perception to an extreme, his friend and fellow painter Alex Katz has pursued possibilities in the opposite direction.

Katz usually develops his large works from small oils, such as *Vincent in Canoe*. Such paintings move successively up in size while going through a process of constant refinement of tone, color, drawing, and subtle compositional shifts. Katz has brought to Realism the scale of abstract painting and the immediacy of recognition typical of Pop Art.

These modern icon/images serve as a stylish record of his personal life: wife, son, dog, studio, and cottage marked by the change of time, age, and circumstance; his friends: artists, poets, dealers, and dancers; and events: a quiet moment between friends, canoeing or swimming, a cocktail party, an opening or performance. The body of Katz's work — paintings, prints, and the unique cutouts — stands as a document of contemporary life narrated by a painter.

While Katz is the most modern, Jack Beal is the most expressionistic and psychologically penetrating of the Realists. He is given to advocating extreme positions which change periodically. Nevertheless, each esthetic shift has provided remarkable results in his paintings.

The Still Life Painter, which Beal produced for *The Big Still Life* exhibition at the Allan Frumkin Gallery, depicts the artist's wife, Sondra Freckleton, at work on a still life watercolor. Beal's painting and Freckleton's watercolor which appears in it were exhibited together in the exhibition. They illustrate the different intentions and preoccupations of each painter. The quilts, compote, and bric-a-brac come from their weekend visits to rural flea markets near their farm. The begonia, which serves as the focal point of *The Still Life Painter,* is one of the many varieties tended by Sondra and which appear frequently in her work and Beal's.

Beal had just returned from his second trip to Europe, and this painting represents a fusion of his preoccupation with Dutch painting (particularly the rich chiaroscuro), American artifacts, and the taut, abstract spatial composition derived from Abstract Expressionism, particularly Hans Hoffman's concept of "clam-shell" space.

With work such as *The Still Life Painter,* Beal gives contemporary proof that enigma and drama stem from the attitudinal stance of the painter rather than dictates of the subject.

Wayne Thiebaud for many years was wrongly classified as a Pop artist, primarily because of his choice of still life subjects: pies, cakes, hamburgers, and gum ball machines.

More accurately, Thiebaud reflects the West Coast figurative stance brought to prominence by artists such as David Park, Elmer Bischoff and Richard Diebenkorn. Unlike the East Coast figurative painters of the fifties and sixties, whose subjects were always highly specific, the West Coast figuration is generalized and more abstract in its use of color and light.

Thiebaud takes the contemporary foods and objects so highly reflective of our society and life style and uses them as archtypes. A slice of lemon pie looks the same (it is a calculated and cultivated appearance) in San Francisco, St. Louis, and Miami. Undeniably, his paintings are witty social comments, loaded with double-entendre. His use of paint and color are highly seductive, and it is easy to overlook the subtle moves of space and planes which are more akin to Van Gogh and Morandi than to Pop Art.

The ambiguous landscapes are compositionally structured like Thiebaud's dressing tables with hand mirrors and lipsticks, with the shift of objects conveying the enlargement of scale: mirror to pond, lipstick to tree, and so on. Thiebaud's forays into landscape painting, including the recent San Francisco cityscapes, seems to refer with wit and irony to our subjective perception rather than to the more traditional conception of space.

By comparison, there is the striking contrast of Neil Welliver's painting: Welliver paints what he sees, knows, and protects. His landscapes of northern Maine, deep vistas and dense woods, seem never to have been intruded upon by man. They reflect the excesses of nature within its ability to provide and maintain its own delicate balance. Welliver's is not the idealized pre-Darwinian view of the natural sublime. It is an intelligent and concerned view, a landscape jealously guarded from the ecological disasters of our time.

Like Welliver, John Button, Jane Freilicher, and George Nick were close to Fairfield Porter. Their work has remained painterly while Beal, Pearlstein, and Leslie have moved from painterly to a more visually articulate method.

John Button, best known for his romantic skies seen from lower Manhattan, is originally from the West Coast. He has produced equally remarkable pieces of pure landscape, such as *Lassen County.* Button is a superb and delicate colorist with a surprising command of tone. His careful balance of sky and topography is at once a highly articulate rendering of positive and negative forms. These dramatic spatial compositions, apparent in the large oils and the small gouaches from which the large oils are worked up, are reminiscent of such earlier West Coast abstractions as those of Clifford Still.

Jane Freilicher, by comparison, relies on the traditional device of receding planes for constructing her landscape paintings. Freilicher appears to derive a great deal of sensual, physical pleasure from the act of painting, which may be due to her roots in abstraction. Like the works of Thiebaud, Welliver, and Porter, her paintings reflect the dual nature of the physical propensity of the medium and its possibilities for visual description.

Best known for his paintings of Victorian houses and the suburbs of New England, George Nick is a highly productive chronicler of the urban landscape, an endeavor dominated today by the Photo-Realists. Nick works from direct observation. In this country, a large truck with a skylight and picture window serves as his movable studio. Each painting is more than a record of architecture. It is an accurate description of a structure as articulated by the particularities of seasonal light at a specific hour. According to Nick, studying with Edwin Dickenson served as more useful preparation to this end than his years of solving Albers' abstract color problems at Yale.

It is the combined nuance of season and weather affecting the light (as well as the fact that they are obviously painted) that separates the look of Nick's work from that of the vast majority of the Photo-Realists. Quite simply, the eye can rove,

probe, change aperture and focus. Esthetics aside, direct observation in painting is similar in effect to superimposing many photographs on one image. The resulting impression is literally a collage of information not subject to the limitations of one myopic view. Focus, space, and light are perceived quite differently by the eye than through the lens of a camera.

Another interesting aspect of Nick's architectural subjects is that he has never limited the range of his interests to certain types of structures. He is apt to paint anything. His work includes interiors, portraits, still lifes, and landscapes, though these are simply less frequently exhibited.

A compulsive tourist and traveler, Nick is unique in having produced a large body of work abroad, such as *Portal of San Pablo,* and small paintings (there are no independent drawings) such as *Piazza del Popolo.* There is a distinctly American sensibility, steeped in this country's esthetics, behind the rendering of these European subjects.

The still life, regardless of the degree of adherence to visual fact, offers to the painter an open-ended range of possibilities. No other category of subject matter has such broad appeal to both painter and viewer.

William Bailey is noted for his serious, highly ordered, and quietly mysterious still-life paintings. His collection of crocks and containers would never catch one's eye. Their most striking characteristic is their lack of notability. Commonplace utilitarianism with minor concessions to decoration, design, and color give them a modest grace. They were made primarily to hold things.

And yet, when arranged on Baily's shelf and bathed in that indescribable light, the combination of forms, tactile shifts, and modulation of tones, the ordinary objects so carefully placed and tenderly modeled, take on a quiet mystery that is comparable to Morandi. There is a dignity in these paintings, such as *Manfroni Still Life,* but there is also that rare combination of classicism and poetry.

John Moore brings the same sense of order to his paintings, but his use of space, color, and placement of objects, particularly in the watercolors, is more abstract and patterned. In this way, while distinctly American, his paintings are reminiscent of Japanese prints. Subtle color combinations, transparent and translucent surfaces, and the delicately balanced perspective lead to a reading that fluctuates between literalism and abstraction. *Downtown* is an intellectual and perceptual *tour de force.*

There is a junkiness about the objects selected by Janet Fish that is noteworthy. It is not that quality that incites her to paint them, but it certainly instills them with a familiar charm. These are the objects long ago abandoned by our parents, sent either to the trash bin or the thrift shop as they moved into post-war prosperity. These inexpensive items — colorful glass and Fiesta Ware from the hard times of the Depression — were discarded because they were cheap and were a constant reminder of that gloomy period. For our generation they have a nostalgic and sentimental value, being connected to our childhood and simpler times without the connotations of hardship.

Janet Fish paints objects transformed by light. With this preoccupation there is a drastic shift of emphasis, as distinct as the low line of horizon in Dutch landscapes reflecting the Dutch concern with the weather, to the rendering of light instead of form. Most likely while studying at Yale, she executed the color problems designed by Albers to depict transparency with opaque Color Aid paper and transposed that abstract information to still-life painting. This is not at all what Albers had in mind.

Her recent works are more broadly painted, and the objects are not as crowded into the perimeters of the canvas as in the earlier works. And there is now a confidence and authority that comes only with maturity and experience.

While her depiction of light has references to Impressionism, the use of backlight comes more from photography, and the vigorous use of opaque paint has roots in Expressionism and abstraction. There is little question that enlarging the scale of objects (once considered taboo) comes from Georgia O'Keefe. Such mergers and reverence for the subject are typical of the Realists.

Janet Fish, George Nick, Chuck Close, Rackstraw Downes, Joseph Raffael, Nancy Graves, Richard Serra, Stephen Posen, and other notable artists attended graduate school at Yale at the same time, surely the most exceptional group of talent any art school has produced for decades. Most of them, George Nick an exception, worked in an Abstract Expressionist mode as students, but even this partial list shows that there is an extremely broad range in their mature work.

Stephen Posen's work is a complex mix. In many ways his painting is a collision of improbabilities, always checked by his keen intellect and immense skills as a painter. His very modern *trompe l'oelis,* such as *Boundary,* are more than a display of virtuosity with a fool-the-eye intent. Posen questions and examines the way we perceive, optically and intellectually, the illusion of space, then proceeds to push the problem to extremely ambiguous ends. Though often confused with Photo-Realism, his paintings are scrupulously direct visual observations.

His earlier work was begun from small abstract collages, enlarged by sewing together fabric of the same color. These constructions were fastened to the wall and stuffed with cardboard boxes until the abstractly patterned fabric bulged quite literally into a Cubist relief.

Boundary, a more recent piece, was begun by enlarging a black and white photograph to the size of the canvas and stapling it to the wall. Then strips of colored fabric were fixed to the photographic blow-up, some in correspondence with the composition of the image and others in contradiction to it.

We are conditioned to interpret as three-dimensional space the crudest black and white photograph, and Posen makes use of that response. With the transposition to painting of the photographic image and real cloth, the two distinctly separate illusions flutter together ambiguously. The colored cloth fragments waver between the flat physical surface of the photograph's plane and the illusionistic space contained in the depth of its image.

Such complex juggling would never succeed if Posen were less skillful as a draftsman, colorist, and painter, and would never reach such enigmatic fruition if he were satisfied with the manipulation of those skills as an end.

The danger in looking at works of art in reproduction is that it is easy to be misled into thinking that we really know what they look like. It is a good idea to remember that shock of encountering a Van Eyck, a Goya portrait, a late Van Gogh, or a Matisse cutout for the first time. The more extraordinary the painting technique, the greater the losses in reproduction.

Richard Estes and William Beckman suffer more than most contemporary artists in this regard in that their work ends up looking like photographs, even though Estes (discussed later) is in fact quite painterly and Beckman achieves a luminosity and richness of color and tone that quite simply cannot be reproduced photomechanically.

Beckman is noted for the life-size, scrupulously observed paintings of his wife and for his self-portraits. Working six months to a year on a painting, as he does, necessitates a close involvement with the model, and it is nearly impossible to hire a model for such strenuous sittings over lengthy periods (eight to ten hours daily). Also, Beckman is preoccupied with the alterations of physical appearance as it is modified by the emotional experience of the painter and the subject.

He paints on panels using the old device of a stringed grid in front of the subject; each day he sands down the painted surface, which is built up in thin, successive layers.

Reared on a farm in Minnesota, Beckman has a deep attachment to the land, which is reflected in his landscapes. He speaks of Constable with fascination and deep respect. The landscapes are based on meticulous drawings and highly developed pastels, also drawn through a string grid. Like Vermeer's *View of Delft,* they depict transient light. The clouds are a montage based on sketches and memory with minute attention given to the subtle color changes in the reflective tone and color of the interaction between land and sky. An important aspect of Beckman's landscape is that it depicts the countryside as inhabited and altered by man.

From Thiebaud, Pearlstein, Katz, and Leslie through Fish, Posen, and Beckman, one can trace a cross section of contemporary American life; their use of traditional themes — landscape, portrait, narrative, and still life — is a lucid and evocative reflection of the temper of our time.

17

William Bailey/Biography – 19

HEAD OF A GIRL (1975) – 34
Pencil on paper, 14 × 11 in.
Courtesy: Robert Schoelkopf Gallery,
New York, New York

MANFRONI STILL LIFE (1978) – 35
Oil on canvas, 44⅞ × 57½ in.
Courtesy: The Herbert W. Plimpton Collection,
on extended loan to the Rose Art Museum,
Brandeis University, Massachusetts,
Waltham, Massachusetts

Jack Beal/Biography – 20

PORTRAIT OF JOHN ARTHUR (1976) – 36
Charcoal on paper, 25 × 19 in.
Courtesy: Private Collection

STILL LIFE PAINTER (1978-79) – 37
Oil on canvas, 49¾ × 60 in.
Courtesy: The Toledo Museum of Art,
Gift of Edward Drummond Libbey,
Toledo, Ohio

William Beckman/Biography – 21

CENTRAL HUDSON (1980) – 38
Pastel on paper, 27 × 35½ in.
Courtesy: Allan Stone Gallery, New York,
New York

PARSHALL'S BARN (1977) – 39
Oil on canvas, 63 × 72 in.
Courtesy: Allan Stone Gallery, New York,
New York

John Button/Biography – 22

23RD STREET HIGH NOON (1978) – 40
Gouache on paper, 19¾ × 26¾ in.
Courtesy: Fischbach Gallery, New York,
New York

LASSEN COUNTY, CALIFORNIA (1980) – 41
Oil on canvas, 60 × 84 in.
Courtesy: Fischbach Gallery, New York,
New York

Janet Fish/Biography – 23

SPOONS AND CARNATIONS (1979) – 42
Pastel on paper, 26 × 30¼ in.
Courtesy: Robert Miller Gallery, New York,
New York

ORANGE BOWLS AND YELLOW – 43
PITCHER (1979)
Oil on canvas, 60 × 70 in.
Courtesy: Robert Miller Gallery, New York,
New York

Jane Freilicher/Biography – 24

PEONY (1979) – 44
Pastel on paper, 4½ × 6½ in.
Courtesy: Fischbach Gallery, New York,
New York

DUNES, POND, MARSH (1976) – 45
Oil on canvas, 66 × 50 in.
Courtesy: Fischbach Gallery, New York,
New York

Alex Katz/Biography – 25

VINCENT IN CANOE (1974) – 46
Oil on masonite, 16 × 16¼ in.
Courtesy: Harcus Krakow Gallery, Boston,
Massachusetts

DOROTHY (1974) – 47
Oil on canvas, 48 × 60 in.
Courtesy: Marlborough Gallery, Inc.,
New York, New York

Alfred Leslie/Biography – 26

REBECCA WERNER (1978) – 48
Graphite on paper, 40 × 30 in.
Courtesy: Allan Frumkin Gallery, New York,
New York

SEVEN A.M. NEWS (1976-78) – 49
Oil on canvas, 84 × 60 in.
Courtesy: Joseph Shein, Philadelphia,
Pennsylvania

John Moore/Biography – 27

UNTITLED (#131) (1980) – 50
Watercolor on paper, 30 × 22½ in.
Courtesy: Fischbach Gallery, New York,
New York

DOWNTOWN (1978) – 51
Oil on canvas, 96 × 36 in.
Courtesy: Fischbach Gallery, New York,
New York

George Nick/Biography – 28

PIAZZA DEL POPOLO (1971) – 52
Oil on canvas, 11¾ × 10 in.
Courtesy: George Nick,
Boston, Massachusetts

PORTAL OF SAN PABLO, CORDOBA,
SPAIN (1979) – 53
Oil on canvas, 40 × 30 in.
Courtesy: Tibor de Nagy Gallery, New York,
New York

Philip Pearlstein/Biography – 29

TWO FEMALE MODELS, SEATED AND
RECLINING ON INDIAN RUG (1975) – 54
Sepia wash on paper, 29½ × 41 in.
Courtesy: Allan Frumkin Gallery, New York,
New York

FEMALE MODEL ON CHIEF'S BLANKET (1976) – 55
Oil on canvas, 60 × 72 in.
Courtesy: Allan Frumkin Gallery, New York,
New York

Fairfield Porter/Biography – 30

SUN AND SEA (ca. 1974) – 56
Watercolor on paper, 30 × 22½ in.
Courtesy: Hirschl & Adler Galleries, Inc.,
New York, New York

COLUMBUS DAY (1968) – 57
Oil on canvas, 80 × 80 in.
Courtesy: Tibor de Nagy Gallery, New York,
New York

Stephen Posen/Biography – 31

UNTITLED (1973) – 58
Graphite on paper, 40 × 30 in.
Courtesy: Stephen Posen,
New York, New York

BOUNDARY (1977-78) – 59
Oil on canvas, 72 × 90 in.
Courtesy: Robert Miller Gallery, New York,
New York

Wayne Thiebaud/Biography – 32

STILL LIFE WITH BOWL (1970) – 60
Charcoal on paper, 18 × 22 in.
Courtesy: Charles Campbell Gallery,
San Francisco, California

RIVER POND (1967-75) – 61
Acrylic on canvas, 60 × 78 in.
Courtesy: Memorial Art Gallery of the University
of Rochester, Joseph C. Wilson Memorial Fund,
Rochester, New York

Neil Welliver/Biography – 33

STUDY FOR "DEER" (1980) – 62
Watercolor on paper, 22½ × 25½ in.
Courtesy: Brooke Alexander, Inc., New York,
New York

PROSPECT BROOK (1978) – 63
Oil on canvas, 96 × 96 in.
Courtesy: Stephen S. Alpert, Wayland,
Massachusetts

WILLIAM BAILEY

Born: Council Bluffs, Iowa, 1930

Education: University of Kansas, Yale University

Current Residence: New Haven, Connecticut

Selected Exhibitions:

Solo

• Robert Schoelkopf Gallery, New York City, 1968, 1971, 1974, 1979

• Galleria Dei Lanzi, Milan, 1973 • Galleria Il Fante di Spade, Rome, 1973 • Galleria La Parisina, Turin, 1973

• Galerie Claude Bernard, Paris, 1978

Group

• "Three Centuries of the American Nude", New York Cultural Center, 1975

• "Realism Now", Vassar College Art Gallery, 1968 • "America the Third Century", 1976

• "American Academy in Rome: Five Painters", Union Carbide Bldg., New York City, 1978

• "Artists Choose: Figurative/Realist Art", Artists' Choice Museum, New York City, 1979

Represented by Robert Schoelkopf Gallery, New York City

JACK BEAL

Born: Richmond, Virginia, 1931

Education: William & Mary College, Art Institute of Chicago, University of Chicago

Current Residence: New York City and Oneonta, New York

Selected Exhibitions:

Solo

• Allan Frumkin Gallery, New York City, 1965, 1967, 1968, 1970, 1972, 1973, 1975, 1978, 1980

• Retrospective Exhibition, The Virginia Museum, Boston University and Museum of Contemporary Art, Chicago, 1974

Group

• "Realism Now", Vassar College Art Gallery, 1968 • "22 Realists", Whitney Museum of American Art, 1970

• "The American Landscape", Boston University, 1972 • "America 1976", U.S. Department of the Interior, 1976

• "Seven on the Figure", the Pennsylvania Academy of the Fine Arts, 1979

• "Direction in Realism", Danforth Museum, Framingham, MA, 1980

Represented by Allan Frumkin Gallery, New York City

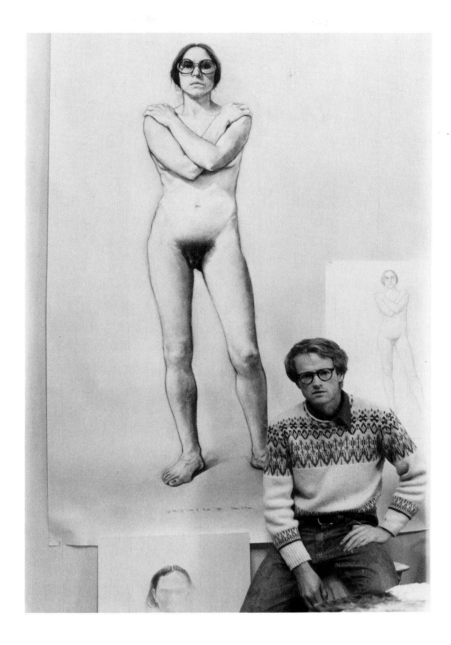

WILLIAM BECKMAN

Born: Minnesota, 1942

Education: State University at St. Cloud, University of Iowa

Current Residence: Wassaic, New York

Selected Exhibitions:

Solo

• Hudson River Museum, New York, 1969 • Allan Stone Gallery, 1970, 1971, 1974, 1976

Group

• Art Institute of Chicago, 1974 • "Aspects of the Figure", the Cleveland Museum, 1974

• "Trends in Contemporary Realist Painting", Museum of Fine Arts, Boston, 1975

• Wildenstein, Inc., New York City, 1976

Represented by Allan Stone Gallery, New York City

JOHN BUTTON

Born: San Francisco, California, 1929

Education: University of California at Berkeley, California School of Fine Art, University of California Medical Center,

Howard Warshaw, Altina Barrett, Willard Cummings

Selected Exhibitions:

Solo

• Tibor de Nagy Gallery, New York City, 1956-1959

• Kornblee Gallery, New York City, 1963-1974 • Fischbach Gallery, New York City, 1978, 1980

Group

• "Realism Now", Vassar College Art Gallery, 1968 • "Eight Landscape Painters", Museum of Modern Art, 1965

• "Painterly Realism", American Federation of Arts, 1970 • "New York Now", Phoenix Art Museum, 1979

Represented by Fischbach Gallery, New York City

JANET FISH

Born: Boston, Massachusetts, 1938

Education: Smith College, Yale University

Current Residence: New York City

Selected Exhibitions:

Solo

• Kornblee Gallery, New York City, 1971, 1972, 1973, 1974, 1975, 1976

• Robert Miller Gallery, New York City, 1978, 1979 • University of New York at Stony Brook, 1978

Group

• "8 Contemporary American Realists", the Pennsylvania Academy of the Fine Arts, 1977

• "Born in Boston", De Cordova Museum, 1979 • "Selections from Skowhegan", University of Maryland Art Gallery, 1979

• "Waterworks", University of North Dakota Art Galleries, 1979-1980

Represented by Robert Miller Gallery, Inc., New York City

JANE FREILICHER

Born: New York City, 1924

Education: Brooklyn College, Columbia University, Hans Hoffman School of Fine Arts

Current Residence: New York City

Selected Exhibitions:

Solo

• The Wadsworth Atheneum, Hartford, Connecticut, 1976-1977

• Fischbach Gallery, New York City, 1975, 1977, 1979 • Utah Museum of Fine Arts, University of Utah

Group

• "A Sense of Place", Sheldon Memorial Art Gallery, University of Nebraska, 1973

• "Invitational Award Exhibitions", The American Academy of Arts and Letters, New York City, 1975 • "America, 1976", U.S. Department of the Interior, 1976

• "Artists Salute Skowhegan", Kennedy Galleries, New York City, 1977 • "Poets and Painters", Denver Art Museum, 1979

Represented by Fischbach Gallery, New York City

ALEX KATZ

Born: New York City, 1927

Education: Cooper Union, Skowhegan School of Painting and Sculpture

Current Residence: New York City

Selected Exhibitions:

Solo

• Marlborough Gallery, New York City, 1973, 1976, 1978

• American Foundation for the Arts, Miami, Florida, 1976 • Fresno Arts Center, Fresno, California (and tour to U.C., Long Beach,

Seattle Art Museum, Art Gallery of Greater Victoria, Portland Center for the Visual Arts), 1977-1978

• Rose Art Museum, Brandeis University, 1978 • Queens Museum, Flushing, New York, 1980

Represented by Marlborough Gallery, New York City

ALFRED LESLIE

Born: Bronx, New York, 1927

Education: New York University, Art Students League

Current Residence: New York City

Selected Exhibitions:

Solo

• Museum of Fine Arts, Boston, Hirshorn Museum, Museum of Contemporary Art, Chicago, 1976-1977

• Allan Frumkin Gallery, Chicago (drawings), 1977

Group

• "America '76", U.S. Department of the Interior, 1976 • "Nothing But Nudes", Whitney Museum of American Art, 1977

• "Drawings of the '70s", Museum of Modern Art, 1977 • "Late Twentieth Century Art: The Sydney and Frances Lewis Foundation",

Anderson Gallery, Virginia Commonwealth University, 1978-1979

Represented by Allan Frumkin Gallery, New York City

JOHN MOORE

Born: St. Louis, Missouri, 1941

Education: Washington University, Yale University

Selected Exhibitions:

Solo

• Fischbach Gallery, New York City, 1973, 1975, 1978, 1980

• Pennsylvania Academy of the Fine Arts, 1973 • University of Missouri, St. Louis, 1978

Group

• "At the Academy", Pennsylvania Academy of the Fine Arts, 1976 • "Still Life", Boston University Art Gallery

• "Artists Salute Skowhegan", Kennedy Gallery, New York City, 1977 • "American Realists", Clarke-Benton Gallery, Santa Fe, New Mexico, 1977

• "American Realism", William and Mary College, Williamsburg, Virginia, 1978 • "The Big Still Life", Frumkin Gallery, New York City, 1979

• "Contemporary Naturalism: Work of the 1970s", Nassam County Museum of Fine Art, New York, 1980

Represented by Fischbach Gallery, New York City

GEORGE NICK

Born: Rochester, New York, 1927

Education: Cleveland Institute of Art, Brooklyn Museum Art School, Art Students League, Yale University

Current Residence: Boston, Massachusetts

Selected Exhibitions:

Solo

• Tibor de Nagy Gallery, 1977, 1978, 1979-1980

• Harcus-Karkow Gallery, 1974, 1979 • Richard Gray Gallery, 1969, 1972, 1974, 1977

• Schoelkopf Gallery, 1965, 1967 • Carnegie Institute, Museum of Art, Pittsburgh, Pennsylvania, 1964

Group

• "America 1976", U.S. Department of the Interior, 1976 • "Painterly Realism", Houston, Tulsa, Waco, 1978-1979

• "Things Seen", Sheldon Memorial Art Gallery, University of Nebraska, 1978-1979

Represented by Tibor de Nagy Gallery, Inc., New York City

PHILIP PEARLSTEIN

Born: Pittsburgh, Pennsylvania, 1924

Education: Carnegie Institute of Technology, New York University

Current Residence: New York City

Selected Exhibitions

Solo

• Allan Frumkin Gallery, New York City, 1962, 1963, 1965, 1967, 1969, 1972, 1974, 1976, 1978

• Georgia Museum of Art, University of Georgia (also Wichita Museum of Art and Vassar College Museum), 1970-1971

• Staatliche Museen-Kupferstichkabinett, Berlin and Kunstverein, Hamburg, 1972 • Finch College Museum, New York, 1974 (toured during 1974 and 1975) • Neuberger Museum, SUNY, Purchase, New York, 1975

• Springfield Art Museum, Springfield, Missouri, 1978 • Carnegie-Mellon University, Pittsburgh, Pennsylvania, 1979

Group

• "Realismus and Realitat", Kunsthalle, Darmstadt, 1975 • Whitney Biennial Exhibition, New York City, 1979

• "Figurative/Realist Art", Artists Choice Museum, 1979

Represented by Allan Frumkin Gallery, New York City

FAIRFIELD PORTER

1907-1975

Education: Harvard College, the Art Students League

Selected Exhibitions:

• Tibor de Nagy Gallery, fifteen exhibitions between 1952 and 1970

• The Parrish Art Museum, Southampton, New York, 1971, 1977 • Hirschl and Adler Galleries, New York, 1972, 1974, 1976

• Kent State University, Kent, Ohio, 1967 • Cleveland Museum of Art, Cleveland, Ohio, 1966 • Reed College, Portland, Oregon, 1965

• Rhode Island School of Design, Providence, Rhode Island, 1959

Fairfield Porter's work is represented in many museum collections, including the Metropolitan Museum of Art,
the Museum of Modern Art, the Whitney Museum of American Art, the Wadsworth Atheneum, the Cleveland Museum of Art,
the Dayton Art Institute and the Hirshorn Museum. Mr. Porter's book, *Thomas Easkins,* was published by Braziller in 1959.
He was a frequent contributor to *Art in America, Art News, The Nation,* and the *Evergreen Review.*
He taught or was visiting artist at Yale University, the Skowhegan School of Painting and Sculpture,
the Maryland Institute, Amherst College and the Art Institute of Chicago.

Represented by Hirschl and Adler Galleries, New York City

STEPHEN POSEN

Born: St. Louis, Missouri, 1939

Education: Washington University, Yale University

Current Residence: New York City

Selected Exhibitions:

Solo

• Robert Miller Gallery, New York City, 1978

• O. K. Harris Works of Art, New York City, 1969, 1970, 1971, 1974

Group

• "Illusion and Reality", Canberra, Australian National Gallery (and tour throughout Australia), 1977-1978

• "Malerie Und Photographie Im Dialog", Zurich, Kunsthaus, 1977

• "Eight Contemporary American Realists", Pennsylvania Academy of the Fine Arts, 1977

Represented by Robert Miller Gallery, Inc., New York City

WAYNE THIEBAUD

Born: Mesa, Arizona, 1920

Education: Sacramento State College

Current Residence: Sacramento, California

Selected Exhibitions:

Solo

• Crocker Art Gallery, Sacramento, California, 1952, 1970

• De Young Museum, San Francisco, 1962 • Retrospective Exhibition, Phoenix Art Museum
(tour to Oakland Museum, Des Moines Art Center, Neuberger Museum, Museum of Fine Arts, Boston), 1977

Group

• "American Master Drawings & Watercolors", American Federation of Arts, 1976-1977

• "Eight from California", National Collection of Fine Arts, 1974

• "Living American Artists and the Figures", Museum of Art, Pennsylvania State University, 1974-1975

• "Aspects of the Figure", the Cleveland Museum of Art, 1974

Represented by Allan Stone Gallery, New York City

NEIL WELLIVER

Born: Millville, Pennsylvania, 1929

Education: Philadelphia Museum College of Art, Yale University

Current Residence: Lincolnville, Maine

Selected Exhibitions:

Solo

• University of Rhode Island, 1974 • Fischbach Gallery, New York City, 1974, 1976, 1979, 1980

Group

• "First International Biennial of Figurative Painting", Tokyo and Osaka, 1975

• "Candid Painting: American Genre", DeCordova Museum, Lincoln, Massachusetts, 1975

• "America, 1976", U.S. Department of the Interior, 1976 • "Artists Salute Skowhegan", Kennedy Galleries, New York City, 1977

• "Late Twentieth Century Art", the Sydney and Frances Lewis Collection, I.C.A. Gallery, New York City, 1979

• "The Decade in Review: Selections from the 1970s", Whitney Museum of American Art, 1979

Represented by Fischbach Gallery, New York City

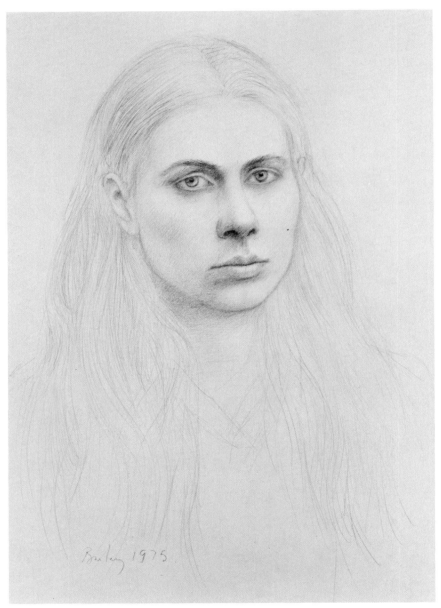

Head of a Girl (1975)

Manfroni Still Life (1978)

Portrait of John Arthur (1976)

Still Life Painter (1978-79)

Central Hudson (1980)

Parshall's Barn (1977)

23rd Street High Noon (1978)

Lassen County, California (1980)

Spoons and Carnations (1979)

Orange Bowls and Yellow Pitcher (1979)

Peony (1979)

Dunes, Pond, Marsh (1976)

Vincent in Canoe (1974)

Dorothy (1974)

Rebecca Werner (1978)

Seven A.M. News (1976-78)

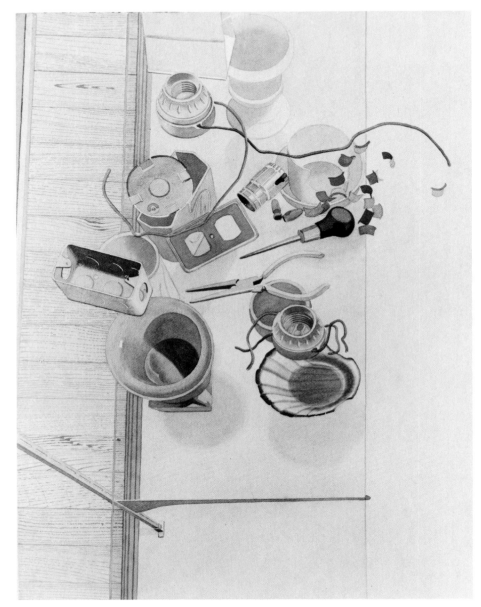

Untitled (#131) (1980)

Downtown (1978)

Piazza Del Popolo (1971)

Portal of San Pablo, Cordoba, Spain (1979)

Two Female Models, Seated and Reclining on Indian Rug (1975)

Female Model on Chief's Blanket (1976)

Sun and Sea (ca. 1974)

Columbus Day (1968)

Untitled (1973)

Boundary (1977-78)

Still Life with Bowl (1970)

River Pond (1967-75)

Study for "Deer" (1980)

Prospect Brook (1978)

PHOTOREALISM

I am labeled a Photo-Realist because I use a photograph to do a realistic-looking painting. However, the camera is an extension of my eyes, of myself. My paintings look photographic, but they are not photographic. They are pure painting. I paint the landscape, or part of it, and I represent an image that impresses me. Impression and Expression. Very simple.

John Baeder, *Diners,* by John Baeder, Harry N. Abrams, Inc., New York

The abstract quality of reality is far more exciting than most of the abstract painting that I see.

Richard Estes, *Richard Estes: The Urban Landscape,* John Canaday and John Arthur, Museum of Fine Arts, Boston, and New York Graphic Society, Boston, 1978

The recent explosion of interest in photography, and the concurrent rapid rise in the prices paid for photographs, is due in part to the growing popularity of Photo-Realism, which has changed our consideration of the photograph, and also to the renewed interest in the Steiglitz group, coupled with a reexamination of the great documentary and journalistic photography of Walker Evans, Dorothea Lange, Berenice Abbott, Russell Lee, and others.

Each of these factors, developing separately, came into prominence with the growing mania for Americana brought on by the celebration of the Bicentennial at a time when the gloomy state of the American political scene provided little cheer.

The symbiotic relationship between painting and photography has been confused because the two have traditionally been discussed separately. As I have written:

"Every painter has used devices and systems. Painters concerned with representation have employed aids for reproducing and reducing the spatial world on a flat surface. Da Vinci discussed pinhole projection . . . and investigated optics, but strangely, never explored the existing possibilities of graphic reproduction, which raises many areas of speculation. Both he and Dürer developed canons of proportion and the latter demonstrated the use of a stringed grid as a means of dealing with the knotty problem of foreshortening.

"When the lens replaced the pinhole far greater clarity and resolution was available for the artist as a means of tracing an image. The addition of ground glass in a portable box led to the marvelous works of Canaletto, Guardi, and when Vermeer set up the camera obscura in the small interior spaces of his home, the lens greatly exaggerated the linear perspective, distorted the relationship of foreground objects to those deeper in the interior, highlights beaded up and when combined with this painter's penchant for transient moments and his Dutch sense of order . . . the resulting images came to be regarded as one of the most remarkable moments in painting.

"It requires little imagination to predict the next, highly obvious step in the use of the camera obscura. A strong part of the compelling urge for the artist trafficking in images is the desire to arrest and hold with specificity, nuance, and brightened emphasis, an engaging momentary vision.

"Once the subject was available with clarity in a darkened box, the next move was to find a means of obtaining a permanent image. This final means sought by the artist was provided by Daguerre, a painter and set designer, in 1839, by placing a light-sensitive copper plate in the camera obscura which became the simultaneous beginning of photography, a new and different art form. In regard to the use of the camera, for the painter it has traditionally provided a means to an end, obtaining accurate, detailed information, while for the photographer the resulting image was an end in itself."

John Arthur, *Realist Drawings and Watercolors,* New York Graphic Society, Boston, 1980

The shock of Photo-Realism in the mid-sixties was two-fold: the paintings looked like photographs, and the artists had chosen subjects from the turf of the street photographer and the photo-journalist, and from advertising.

Howard Kanovitz, Malcolm Morley, and Lowell Nesbitt were three of the first Photo-Realists to emerge on the art scene, Kanovitz recording Manhattan gatherings, Morley with paintings of ocean liners rendered with the glossy look of travel brochures, and Nesbitt with large, dramatic paintings of artists' studios.

Nesbitt has painted practically everything from panoramic landscapes to the shoes in his closet, and his work, unlike much of Photo-Realism, looks hand painted. Without doubt, his most popular and best-known works are the large blow-ups of flowers, such as *Black Parrot Tulip.* The enlarged scale, a device also used by Joseph Raffael, is an avenue opened by O'Keefe, but Nesbitt's flowers, with their flat, complementary colored backgrounds, have the look of photo reproductions from seed packets and gardening catalogues. This is botany enhanced rather than reproduced. Nesbitt's production is staggering, and he is one of the few painters with a staff, including a gardener, to manage his diverse affairs.

The impulse in painting toward a rejuvenation of interest in the urban landscape, with all its contemporary consumer-oriented accoutrements (automobiles, trailers, pickups, motorcycles) had precedents prior to the work of Richard Estes, but no other artist has so heavily shaped and influenced the look of Photo-Realism.

It is ironic that most Photo-Realist painting flooding the art world has arisen from a total misunderstanding of Estes' work, derived from the viewing of reproduction prints rather than the original paintings.

Richard Estes is the most intuitive painter in contemporary Realism; there is more shuffling beneath the surfaces of his pristinely finished paintings than one would suspect.

He does not project slides, and he often uses a wide assortment of color photographs, which he prints himself, of a particular scene. This aspect of his work places him closer to the Realists in that three-dimensional space is not rendered from a single, myopic source.

His only drawings — unfortunately for anyone with an appetite for drawings who has seen an Estes painting in the beginning stages — are beneath his paintings. They are loosely drawn with acrylic wash. The perspective is altered; the proportions of buildings are changed; automobiles appear and disappear; the locations of objects and structures are often shifted. When the underpainting is completed, Estes overpaints with oil. He is a superb colorist with complete tonal control. In the end, his paintings are not at all reproductions of photographs.

His prints follow a similar pattern of construction, from broad, flat colors and shapes to minute detail. Close examination of the window display on the left in *Qualicraft Shoes* reveals a ghostly relief of a fur coat which has been replaced by the existing objects. The silk-screened print also reveals his method of simplifying objects and details giving his work a crispness and clarity that is distinctly different from most Photo-Realist painting, which is not significantly altered or edited from the photographic source material.

It is noteworthy that an Estes painting attracts and enchants, while its real counterpart most often does not. Painting, especially significant painting, alters our response to reality and reexamines our relationship to it.

Leaving a successful career in graphic design to pursue painting full time, Robert Cottingham has chosen the urban iconography of street and storefront advertising. Examined formally, his paintings share the characteristics of polychrome Cubist constructions and Abstract Expressionist assemblages. But there is also wit, charm, and irony in his edited and meticulously composed signs. A cropped fragment spells "Art"; a movie marquee advertises a gruesome and sensational film title, *Black Girl and the Butcher,* but is rated PG;. and in the patriotically colored *Rat* (Cottingham is one of the few Photo-Realists to take liberties with color), the striped

banner covers and abbreviates the name "Rattner's."

Cottingham takes frequent bus trips to various cities (bus stations are usually located in the decaying sections of a city) in order to photograph this peculiar aspect of Americana.

The IRS may question John Baeder's travel expenses, but anyone who knows him, or his book *Diners,* can vouch for the fact that he will go anywhere, anytime, to photograph a diner or fast-food eatery, such as *Deluca's Dining Car, Pittsfield, Mass.,* or the Arcade Snack Deli next to *Honest John's Casino* in Las Vegas.

Baeder is obsessed with all aspects of this rapidly disappearing phenomenon, which has apparently been doomed to extinction by the fast-food chains. He has amassed an enormous collection of memorabilia, postcards, matches, and photographs; he can elaborate on the peculiarities and specialties of each diner's menu and is able to describe in detail the physical and personal quirks of many proprietors. He is not only a skillful painter; he is a notable journalist and documentarian.

A peculiar but explainable aspect of Photo-Realism is the fact that most of its practitioners do not draw. The photograph and transparency have replaced the need for such source material. There is a different intent behind the production of drawings and watercolors, which could more aptly be described as miniature paintings.

Richard Haas develops his large paintings from sketches and photographs, bringing into play considerable skill at architectural rendering. He is extremely knowledgeable in the history of architecture. In addition to a large body of paintings (usually watercolors) and prints, Haas has produced and gained national prominence for his architecturally harmonious wall murals on the exteriors of buildings and his illusionistic manipulations of interior space.

There is an enormous body of work by Haas, and although it focuses exclusively on architecture, his stance is unique in that he has never adhered to a photographic look, and he chooses his subjects for their historic and esthetic relevance.

For Ralph Goings and Robert Bechtle, architecture is used not so much as a subject as a locale, fixing or describing, even in absentia, the regional and class characteristics of its inhabitants. Both artists could be accurately described as "genre" painters.

When Ralph Goings paints a pickup truck or diner still life it is more than an adroit depiction of the subject; it also refers by implication to its users and owners.

His still-life paintings are a far cry from the similar but painterly and witty images of the same subjects by Thiebaud, for Goings incorporates the objective air of his photographs, down to and including the distortions of mechanical focus.

Pee Wee's Diner is not the quaint and ingratiating view of America typified by Norman Rockwell or the romanticized, Republican view of rural life, bathed in the sentimentality of

Andrew Wyeth. It is not the way we want things to be or pretend them to be. Goings paints the small town and its inhabitants as they are.

There is an edge of deep familiarity, a sense of *deja vu,* in the images of Robert Bechtle. These are paintings of small events and minor moments: relatives on the back porch, the family car in the driveway.

Bechtle's paintings and watercolors have the artless quality of an amateur snapshot, dutiful records stored in the back of a drawer for an occasional shared reminiscence.

Close examination of Vermeer's paintings will show them to be not hyper-real but rather simplified for visual emphasis and clarity. For example, the head of a woman is reduced almost to an egg shape. This same sort of clarity through visual economy typifies Bechtle's painting.

Perhaps Jack Mendenhall is also a genre painter. If so, his work is not without ironic comment. It is not a depiction based on the way things are (at least for the vast majority) but rather the commercially motivated pretension aimed at how some hope they will be.

These glitzy, overdone interiors, such as *Mirrored Dressing Room,* reek of materialism more than comfort. They are devoid of clues regarding the personalities of their inhabitants, suggesting only their consumer habits, brought to a cluttered arrangement by the crass decorator or window dresser.

Mendenhall's interiors, often worked up from photographs cut from popular decorating magazines, are artificial habitats replete with middle-class symbols but devoid of individual reference. This is the American home as merchandise.

That the Realists and Photo-Realists have developed great formal and technical skills is readily apparent. Much Photo-Realist painting has the vacuity of proportion and intent of an idiot-savant, long on look and short on personal timbre.

While generalization can result in distortion and misrepresentation, it is probably fair to say that Realists are more concerned with the ramifications of content while the Photo-Realists are more preoccupied with the image and its inherent ironies. The latter concern is more immediately attractive, but it faces greater danger from the distancing of time and its cooling of rapport with the subject.

"A rose is a rose is a rose," but a motorcycle is just a motorcycle.

In terms of technical skills directed toward verisimilitude, Stephen Posen and William Beckman of the Realists and Richard Estes and James Valerio of the Photo-Realists are perhaps the most dazzling. This aspect of their work is often blurred in reproduction. Each of these painters has retained in a discernible but subtle way the clear traces of hand and mind.

Too much has been made of the point that Pop and Photo-Realism maintained the formalist prerequisite of flatness by depicting flat images, the former by painting subjects trans-

posed by graphic and mechanical processes, and the latter by painting from two-dimensional photographs. Many of the Photo-Realists readjust an image in order to compensate for the spatial losses suffered in the use of a myopic lens. Surely the issue of flatness is a concern of the critics rather than the painters.

James Valerio's skills of tactile description and his abilities as a colorist are immense; if these were a dominant factor, he would be at the forefront of Photo-Realism. But the grip of subject matter over technical virtuosity rapidly narrows the audience. In general, the audience for art (particularly the purchasing audience) is inclined toward images it would find attractive in a one-to-one confrontation or toward neutral subjects enhanced by the painter's skill.

These attitudes are typified, although exaggerated, in the collections of the large corporations which are rapidly becoming the chief patrons of the arts. Ironically, corporations prefer the neutrality of formalist abstraction, limiting their figurative acquisitions to landscape and still-life painting. Only rarely will a corporation lean toward a contemporary depiction of a person, regardless of the degree of interpretive neutrality or the minor nature of the role that figure might play in the painting as a whole. The human countenance is too loaded with ramifications — personal, social, and psychological — for corporate tastes. Such acquisitions are left to the avid collector.

The acceptability instead of a chrome-plated hot rod engine, of motorcycles, automobiles, garish contemporary artifacts, the reflective and refractive propensities of glass transposed in paint over those works addressed to the human condition, is a depressing indictment of contemporary concerns and values.

If James Valerio were to paint still life, such as the one produced for *The Big Still Life* exhibit, there is no question that he would be one of America's most successful painters. But when those same skills are focused on a figure or a group of figures engaged in an inexplicable or enigmatic event, their propriety is questioned. The innocence and banality of a card trick, checker game, or cat's cradle is disconcerting when coupled with the clarity, color, and scale of his painting. The squashed ooze of a tomato is readily accepted in a painting while the fatty excess of a thigh is not. This is acceptance based not on verisimilitude but on degrees of attractiveness.

Valerio's view of the contemporary world is perhaps closer to the position of the German filmmakers such as Wenders, Herzog, and Fassbinder, and his enigmatic images rendered with such disconcerting clarity are reminiscent of scenes such as the mindless play with the Polaroid in *The American Friend,* the surreal dancing chicken in the roadside attraction of *Stroszek,* or the search for coins with a metal detector in Malick's recent American classic *Badlands.*

Gail is perhaps the most accessible of Valerio's figure

paintings, for the young woman is attractive, as is the robe, drapery, and Oriental rug. But there is the strange hint of light filtering through the drape suggesting an unanticipated landscape beyond, and the inexplicable goldfish swimming above the woman's head. The various aspects of the image add up to a whole that quivers somewhere between reality and dream.

Joseph Raffael and Ben Schonzeit have moved from their highly descriptive earlier painting methods to a more painterly and expressive form of Photo-Realism. Both project slides on the canvas, but Raffael's technique differs drastically from that of other Photo-Realists.

His romantic themes depict the lush elements of nature: earth, air, and water seemingly unintruded upon by man. Generally, he avoids deep space and vistas in favor of more intimate aspects of nature and, like Lowell Nesbitt, relies on radical enlargements in the scale of the subjects. In size his canvases are more akin to those used by color field painters. Also, Raffael, like Ralph Goings, occasionally incorporates the results of focal length of the lens, with parts of the picture out of focus.

There is a descernable poetic and mystical layer to Raffael's subjects. He is closer, in spite of the clarity of his images, to Redon than Redoute. In regard to the formal and technical aspects of his paintings, Raffael traces in paint the patterns and shapes of the lights and darks rather than the forms of the objects, an intent close to that of an Impressionist such as Monet.

From a distance, his works have the look of Photo-Realism; up close the image fades, dominated by the abstract qualities of the patterns and paint. This fluctuation between abstraction and realism is heightened by the choice of highly abstract subjects such as water, which acquires its visual characteristics from light, reflection, refraction, and movement, wedded to the physical propensity of paint and medium.

In his earlier work, Ben Schonzeit, like Chuck Close, produced the highly specific tactile descriptions typical of the Photo-Realists. Both used the airbrush with astonishing virtuosity and thus avoided any trace of the human hand, or what Close has described as "art marks."

But where Close adheres to a rigid format of large scale, frontal, and expressionless heads enlarged from a gridded photograph and rendered either in monochrome or the four colors used in offset photoreproduction, Schonzeit has been much less programmatic. He has dealt with a broad range of subjects, from plastic-wrapped cauliflower to Western mountain ranges. Where Close has used the grid as a means of transfer and enlargement, Schonzeit paints directly over the projected image in a darkened studio. Also, he uses a wide range of mixed colors in his paintings.

The more recent work by Chuck Close has explored the transfer and codification of information, often with more evidence of the grid, emphasizing the intellectual process and visual perception. Schonzeit has moved away from the use of the airbrush to energetic and expressively painted images such as *Short Stuff,* and variations on a single image, such as the drawing *The Music Room #3.* The image is still constructed over a slide projection, but the precise design of the subject matter with a use of paint that is highly indicative of the act of painting.

It is noteworthy, and somewhat ironic, that major Realist painters such as Beal, Pearlstein, and Leslie have tightened up their painting over the past decade, shifting more to tactile description, while hard-core Photo-Realists such as Malcolm Morley, Chuck Close, Joseph Raffael and Ben Schonzeit have followed the opposite path, moving toward more expressive and suggestive uses of medium and imagery.

For the painter, *trompe l'oeil* is a preoccupation with roots stretching back at least to the frescoes and mosaics of Pompeii. If one accepts the dubious argument that Photo-Realism is a depiction of a two-dimensional photographic image, then most of the paintings in that mode can be considered as *trompe l'oeil*

John Clem Clarke, from his earliest variations on the Old Masters, has produced ironic *trompe l'oeil* interpretations of essentially two-dimensional objects. By the late sixties, Clarke was transforming master paintings from projected slides to rich, tapestry-like reconstructions.

His method involves breaking down the image into patterns of light, dark, and color reminiscent of a paint-by-numbers kit. But Clarke, working usually from darks to lights, produces for each color and tonal pattern a paper stencil similar to those used in the pochoir process, which he sprays through with a paint gun. The end result is a rich, mottled surface very much like a tapestry.

He moved from reworked Old Master paintings to his own variations of classical themes, such as *The Judgment of Paris* and *The Three Graces,* then to surprisingly deceptive take-offs on Abstract Expressionism (his thick, impasto brush-marks were absolutely flat) and constructed facades of dilapidated buildings. Unfortunately, the range of his work has never been catalogued or documented in a survey.

John Clem Clarke's present work incorporates aspects of his past oeuvre. *G Series - News 2,* with its collage of news photographs depicting current events beneath fragments of shattered glass is a low relief construction and painting combined, and is based on the assemblage (page 94) by the artist.

Like John Clem Clarke's paintings, the *trompe l'oeil* paintings by Paul Sarkisian are based on collaged assemblages of specific and recognizable materials such as packages, newspapers, and labels. Such constructions are rooted in early Cubist collages and have a precedent, but as an end in itself, in the work of Francis Picabia, Alfred Leslie, and Robert Rauschenberg. But where their collages were abstractions assembled with "real" materials, Sarkisian's paintings of collaged materials are extremely deceptive, even under close scrutiny. His works bring a witty and ironic close to the inter-related loop between abstraction and Realism.

The conventions of still-life painting have changed very little since its earliest practice, and the genre is still a source of delight. Only the objects and rendering methods change with time, and its confines offer a wide range of expressive and interpretive possibilities.

Don Eddy explores the repeated or similar forms of objects displayed in shop windows. The choice of arrangement is eliminated with the esthetic possibilities narrowed to the decisions of cropping found in compositions of commercial intent. These silver objects are commodities, and only upon purchase do they begin to acquire status as heirlooms. Utility is of minor import; these are expensive, mass-produced gifts, ceremonially marked both in giving and use to denote commemoration of an occasion.

The artifice in the reverberations from these objects is amplified by their repetition to infinity in all directions, seemingly ended only by the perimeters of the canvas. Imagining an equal number of weddings and anniversaries is staggering. Such an image is rampant with extra-esthetic ramifications.

On the formal side, there are interesting comparisons between Don Eddy's *Silverware V for S* and *Orange Bowls and Yellow Pitcher* by Janet Fish. Eddy's silver bowls have no color of their own; they reflect light and color. The similarity of forms and color allows no compositional focus or direction, with the exception of the horizontal shelves. Logic tells us that the space of the display cabinet is relatively shallow, and the effect, heightened by the closed glass doors and the myopic quality of the photograph, is claustrophobic.

The bowls, flowers, and glass in the Janet Fish painting are translucent rather than reflective, and each object and flower is placed in an abstract color arrangement. Also, the objects are arranged rather than found. Her space is three-dimensional and open.

These two paintings are perhaps the clearest evidence of the visual distinctions and informational differences between direct observation and the use of photographic source material. They also provide ample clues in regard to the divergent concerns and sensibilities of the painters within the seemingly narrow confines of the still life.

To close the discussion with Carolyn Brady's watercolor, *Green Table,* is also to indicate a beginning. Temperamentally, Brady is closer to Janet Fish than to Don Eddy. Her interiors have no ironic edge, as in works by Jack Mendenhall, nor are they like Eddy's silverware, commercial objects in claustrophobic enclosures, robbed of uniqueness.

Brady's paintings are autobiographical — symbolic self-portraits or portraits — and like Van Gogh's painting of his bedroom, chair, the chair for Gauguin, or pair of shoes, they resonate with the personality of their user. Her interiors are beyond shelter, and her table settings move past function. They indicate the sensual, esthetic, and intellectual pleasures she derives from her environment.

Painted with control and finesse in the difficult medium of transparent watercolor, her loaded images are never overbearing. They have an easy-to-take beauty, like a Dutch still life or Barbizon landscape.

Carolyn Brady is one of the many younger figurative artists who have abandoned the traditional painting media such as oil, tempera, and acrylic, in favor of the exclusive use of drawing materials — pastel, colored pencil, graphite, silver point or watercolor — but who either produce drawings on the scale of easel paintings and larger or retain the more intimate drawing size while working with fanatical precision and control.

Of the former, Carolyn Brady, Patricia Tobacco Forrester, Sondra Freckleton, and Susan Shatter are a few of the most impressive watercolorists, and in the latter category there are Theo Wujcik, Juan Gonzales, Bill Richards, and Martha Mayer Erlebacher.

The recent revival of Realism has marked a return, with unique and impressive results, to the visual arts tradition of craftsmanship, drawing skills, and formal control.

It is not a revival of academicisms, for the only constant factors in Realism and Photo-Realism are an emphasis on verisimilitude as a foundation for personal vision and the expression of diverse individual concerns through images of contemporary life.

John Baeder/Biography – 73

DELUCA'S DINING CAR,
PITTSFIELD, MASS. (1980) – 88
Watercolor on paper, 18½ × 25½ in.
Courtesy: O. K. Harris Works of Art, New York,
New York

HONEST JOHN'S (1976) – 89
Oil on canvas, 55 × 70 in.
Courtesy: O. K. Harris Works of Art, New York,
New York

Robert Bechtle/Biography – 74

STINSON BEACH COOKOUT (1978) – 90
Watercolor on paper, 10 × 14½ in.
Courtesy: O. K. Harris Works of Art, New York,
New York

STUCCO WALL (1977) – 91
Oil on canvas, 48¾ × 69½ in.
Courtesy: The Sydney and Frances Lewis
Foundation, Richmond, Virginia

Carolyn Brady/Biography – 75

ANEMONES (1980) – 92
Watercolor on paper, 15¾ × 16¼ in.
Courtesy: Nancy Hoffman Gallery, New York,
New York

GREEN TABLE (1979) – 93
Oil on canvas, 40½ × 28½ in.
Courtesy: Nancy Hoffman Gallery, New York,
New York

John Clem Clarke/Biography – 76

STUDY FOR "G SERIES-NEWS 2" (1980) – 94
Mixed media, 12¼ × 9 in.
Courtesy: O. K. Harris Works of Art, New York,
New York

G SERIES-NEWS 2 (1980) – 95
Oil on canvas, 80½ × 52 in.
Courtesy: O. K. Harris Works of Art, New York,
New York

Robert Cottingham/Biography – 77

COLD BEER (1980) – 96
Graphite on paper, 14 × 14 in.
Courtesy: Robert Cottingham,
Newtown, Connecticut

RAT (1978) – 97
Oil on canvas, 32 × 32 in.
Courtesy: Stephen S. Alpert, Wayland,
Massachusetts

Don Eddy/Biography – 78

UNTITLED (1976) – 98
Graphite on paper, 12 × 13 in.
Courtesy: Nancy Hoffman Gallery, New York,
New York

SILVERWARE V FOR S (1977) – 99
Acrylic on canvas, 40 × 40 in.
Courtesy: Nancy Hoffman Gallery, New York,
New York

Richard Estes/Biography – 79

QUALICRAFT SHOES (1975) – 100
Silkscreen print, 35½ × 49¼ in.
Courtesy: Private Collection

CENTRAL SAVINGS (1975) – 101
Oil on canvas, 36 × 48 in.
Courtesy: Nelson Gallery-Atkins Museum
(Friends of Art Collection),
Kansas City, Missouri

Ralph Goings/Biography – 80

STILL LIFE WITH MUSTARD (1980) – 102
Watercolor on paper, 9½ × 10 in.
Courtesy: O. K. Harris Works of Art, New York,
New York

PEE WEE'S DINER, WARNERVILLE,
NEW YORK (1977) – 103
Oil on canvas, 48 × 48 in.
Courtesy: The Pollock Family, Waltham,
Massachusetts

Richard Haas/Biography – 81

BEACON STREET (1975) – 104
Watercolor on paper, 23¼ × 16¼ in.
Courtesy: J. and R. Davidson, Boston,
Massachusetts

VIEW NORTH FROM THE EMPIRE STATE
BUILDING (1980) – 105
Watercolor on paper, 28½ × 51 in.
Courtesy: Brooke Alexander, Inc., New York,
New York

Jack Mendenhall/Biography – 82

EVERYTHING MUST BE SOLD! (1975) – 106
Watercolor on paper, 12½ × 18½ in.
Courtesy: O. K. Harris Works of Art, New York,
New York

MIRRORED DRESSING ROOM (1977) – 107
Oil on canvas, 59½ × 72⅜ in.
Courtesy: Virginia Museum of Fine Arts,
Richmond, Virginia

Lowell Nesbitt/Biography – 83

BROOME STREET WINDOW II – '76 (1976) – 108
Pencil on paper, 39 × 28½ in.
Courtesy: Andrew Crispo Gallery, New York,
New York

BLACK PARROT TULIP – '78 (1978) – 109
Oil on canvas, 50 × 70 in.
Courtesy: Andrew Crispo Gallery, New York,
New York

Joseph Raffael/Biography – 84

SCOTTISH BUBBLES (1975) – 110
Ink on paper, 22½ × 30 in.
Courtesy: Nancy Hoffman Gallery, New York,
New York

KONA II (1975) – 111
Oil on canvas, 78 × 114 in.
Courtesy: The Williams Companies,
Tulsa, Oklahoma

Paul Sarkisian/Biography – 85

UNTITLED (Milorganite) (1979) – 112
Acrylic on museum board, 32 × 32 in.
Courtesy: Nancy Hoffman Gallery, New York,
New York

UNTITLED #5 (1978) – 113
Acrylic on canvas, 71½ × 71½ in.
Courtesy: The Herbert W. Plimpton Collection,
on extended loan to the Rose Art Museum,
Brandeis University, Massachusetts,
Waltham, Massachusetts

Ben Schonzeit/Biography – 86

THE MUSIC ROOM #3 (1977) – 114
5B pencil on paper, 30 × 30 in.
Courtesy: Nancy Hoffman Gallery, New York,
New York

SHORT STUFF (1978) – 115
Oil on canvas, 48 × 48 in.
Courtesy: Nancy Hoffman Gallery, New York,
New York

James Valerio/Biography – 87

STILL LIFE (1979) – 116
Charcoal and pencil on paper, 48 × 85 in.
Courtesy: Allan Frumkin Gallery, New York,
New York (not in exhibition)

GAIL (1977) – 117
Oil on canvas, 84 × 72 in.
Courtesy: Stephen S. Alpert, Wayland,
Massachusetts

JOHN BAEDER

Born: South Bend, Indiana, 1938

Education: Auburn University

Current Residence: New York City

Selected Exhibitions:

Solo

• Hundred Acres Gallery, New York City, 1972, 1974, 1976

• Morgan Gallery, Shawnee Mission, Kansas, 1973, 1977 • "Diners by John Baeder", Williams College, 1979

Group

• "Selections in Contemporary Realism", Akron Art Institute, 1974 • "Realismus und Realitat", Kunsthalle, Darmstadt, 1975

• "America as Art", National Collection of Fine Arts, 1976 • "Painting and Sculpture Today", Indianapolis Museum of Art, 1976

• "Recent American Realists", Virginia Museum of Art, 1977

Represented by O. K. Harris Works of Art, New York City

ROBERT BECHTLE

Born: San Francisco, 1932

Education: California College of Arts and Crafts, University of California at Berkeley

Current Residence: Berkeley, California

Selected Exhibitions:

Solo

• San Francisco Museum of Art, 1959, 1964, 1967 • Crocker Art Gallery, Sacramento, 1966, 1973

• Fine Arts Gallery of San Diego, 1973 • O. K. Harris Fine Arts, New York City, 1971, 1974, 1977

Group

• "Radical Realism", Museum of Contemporary Art, Chicago, 1971

• "Documenta", Kassel, 1972 • "Whitney Biennial", Whitney Museum of American Art, 1973

• "New Photo Realism", Wadsworth Atheneum, 1974 • "Super Realism", Baltimore Museum of Art, 1976

• "Illusion and Reality", Australian National Gallery (and tour throughout Australia), 1977-78

• "Reflections of Realism", Albuquerque Museum of Art, History and Science, 1979-80

Represented by O. K. Harris Works of Art, New York City

CAROLYN BRADY

Born: Chickasha, Oklahoma, 1937

Education: Oklahoma State University, University of Oklahoma

Current Residence: Baltimore, Maryland

Selected Exhibitions:

Solo

● Nancy Singer Gallery, St. Louis, 1975

● Art Gallery, University of Rhode Island, 1977 ● Nancy Hoffman Gallery, New York City, 1977, 1980

Group

● "Contemporary Images in Watercolor", Akron Art Institute (and tour to Indianapolis and Rochester, New York), 1976

● "Still Life", Boston University Art Gallery, 1977 ● "Things Seen: The Concept of Realism in 20th Century Painting", Sheldon Memorial Art Gallery, University of Nebraska (and touring), 1978 ● "The New American Still Life", Westmorland County Museum of Art, Greensburg, Pennsylvania, 1979 ● "Contemporary American Still Life", Kent State University, Kent, Ohio, 1980

Represented by Nancy Hoffman Gallery, New York City

JOHN CLEM CLARKE

Born: Bend, Oregon, 1937

Education: Oregon State University, Mexico City College, University of Oregon

Current Residence: New York City

Selected Exhibitions:

Solo

● O. K. Harris Works of Art, New York City, 1970, 1972, 1975, 1977

● Galerie de Gestlo, Hamburg, 1970 ● Deson Gallery, Chicago, 1977 ● Morgan Gallery, Kansas City, 1977

Group

● "Whitney Annual", Whitney Museum of American Art, 1967, 1968 ● "Radical Realism", Contemporary Art Museum, Chicago, 1971

● "Painting and Sculpture Today", Indianapolis Art Museum, 1976 ● "America 1976", U.S. Department of the Interior, 1976

● "Illusion and Reality", Australian National Gallery (and tour throughout Australia), 1977-1978

Represented by O. K. Harris Works of Art, New York City

ROBERT COTTINGHAM

Born: Brooklyn, New York, 1935

Education: Pratt Institute

Current Residence: Newtown, Connecticut

Selected Exhibitions:

Solo

• O. K. Harris Works of Art, 1971, 1974, 1976, 1978

• John Berggruen Gallery, San Francisco, 1976 • Ohio State Fair, Columbus, 1978

Group

• "Radical Realism", Museum of Contemporary Art, Chicago, 1971 • "Documenta 5", Kassel, 1972

• "Photo Realism", Serpentine Gallery, London, 1973 • "Hyperealistes Americains", Centre National d'Art Contemporarain, Paris, 1974

• "Super Realism", Baltimore Museum of Art, 1975 • "America as Art", National Collection of Fine Arts, 1976

• "Art About Art", Whitney Museum of American Art, 1978

Represented by Tomas Segal Gallery, Boston, Massachusetts and Galerie de Gestlo, Cologne, Germany

DON EDDY

Born: Long Beach, California, 1944
Education: Fullerton Junior College, University of Hawaii, University of California at Santa Barbara
Current Residence: New York City
Selected Exhibitions:
Solo
• Molly Barnes Gallery, Los Angeles, 1970, 1971
• Galerie Petit, Paris, 1973 • Nancy Hoffman Gallery of New York City, 1974, 1976, 1979
• Williams College Museum of Art, Williamstown, Massachusetts, 1975
Group
• "Super Realism", Baltimore Museum of Art, 1976
• "Documenta 6", Kassel, 1977 • "Cityscape: '78", Oklahoma Art Center, Oklahoma City
• "Auto-Icons", Downtown Whitney, New York City, 1979

Represented by Nancy Hoffman Gallery, New York City

RICHARD ESTES

Born: Kewanee, Illinois, 1936

Education: Art Institute of Chicago

Current Residence: Northwest Harbor, Maine

Selected Exhibitions:

Solo

• "Richard Estes: the Urban Landscape", Museum of Fine Arts, Boston

(and tour to Hirschorn Museum, Toledo Museum of Art and Nelson-Atkins Museum), 1978

• Museum of Contemporary Art, Chicago, 1974 • Allan Stone Gallery, New York City, 1968, 1969, 1970, 1972, 1974

Group

• "Realism Now", Vassar College Art Gallery, 1968 • "Whitney Annual", Whitney Museum of American Art, 1970

• "Radical Realism", Museum of Contemporary Art, Chicago, 1971 • "36th International Biennial Exhibition", Venice, 1972 • "Documenta 5", Kassel, 1972

• "Photo Realism", Serpentine Gallery, London, 1973 • "Three Realists: Close, Estes, Raffael", Worcester Art Museum, 1974

• "America 1976", U.S. Department of the Interior, 1976

Represented by Allan Stone Gallery, New York City

RALPH GOINGS

Born: Corning, California, 1928

Education: California College of Arts and Crafts, Sacramento State College

Current Residence: Charlotteville, New York

Selected Exhibitions:

Solo

• Artists Cooperative Gallery, Sacramento, California, 1960, 1962, 1968

• O. K. Harris Works of Art, New York City, 1970, 1973, 1977 • Museum of Modern Art, New York City, 1978

Group

• "Directions 2: Aspects of a New Realism", Akron Art Institute, Ohio, 1969

• Milwaukee Art Center, Contemporary Arts Museum, Houston, 1969 • "USA West Coast", Kunstverein, Hamburg/Hannover/Koln/Stuttgart, 1971

• "Documenta", Kassel, 1972

• "Hyperrealistes Americains", Galerie Arditti, Paris, 1973 • "Super Realism", Baltimore Museum of Art, 1975

• "Illusion and Reality", Canberra, Australia, Australian National Gallery (and tour throughout Australia), 1977-1978

• "Representation of America", the Metropolitan Museum of Art, 1978

Represented by O. K. Harris Works of Art, New York City

RICHARD HAAS

Born: Spring Green, Wisconsin, 1936

Education: University of Wisconsin, University of Minnesota

Current Residence: New York City

Selected Exhibitions:

Solo

• Brooke Alexander, Inc., New York City, 1973, 1975, 1977, 1980

• "Trompe L'Oeil, Prints & Boxes", Boston Architectural Center, 1977

• Retrospective Exhibition, Norton Gallery and School of Art, West Palm Beach, Florida, 1977

Group

• "America, 1976", U.S. Department of the Interior, 1976

• "Two Hundred Years of American Printmaking", Minneapolis Institute of Arts and the Whitney Museum of American Art, 1976-1977

• "Reality of Illusion", University of Southern California and the Walker Art Center, 1979-1980 • "Artists on Picasso", Walker Art Center, 1980

Richard Haas has executed major wall projects in New York City, Galveston, Boston, Cambridge, Munich and Chicago

Represented by Brooke Alexander, Inc., New York City

JACK MENDENHALL

Born: Ventura, California, 1937

Education: California College of Arts and Crafts

Current Residence: Oakland, California

Selected Exhibitions:

Solo

● O. K. Harris Works of Art, New York City, 1974, 1979

Group

● "New Realism: Modern Art Form", The Boise Gallery of Art, Boise, Idaho, 1977

● "Photo Realism", Museum of Fine Arts, St. Petersberg, Florida, 1977-1978

● "Reflections of Realism", Albuquerque Museum of Art, History and Science, Albuquerque, New Mexico, 1978-1980

● "Collector's Choice", Mississippi Art Association, Museum of Art, Jackson, Mississippi, 1979-1980

● "Interiors", Sumit Art Center, New Jersey, 1979-1980

Represented by O. K. Harris Works of Art, New York City

LOWELL NESBITT

Born: Baltimore, Maryland, 1933

Education: Tyler School of Fine Art, Royal College of Art (London)

Current Residence: New York City

Selected Exhibitions:

Solo

• Baltimore Museum of Art, 1958, 1969 • Corcoran Gallery of Art, 1964, 1973, 1975

• Memorial Art Gallery, University of Rochester, New York, 1975 • Treasure Island Bicentennial Museum, San Francisco, 1976

• Ulrich Museum of Art, Wichita, Kansas, 1977 • Kent State University, Kent, Ohio, 1978

• Andrew Crispo Gallery, New York City, 1975, 1977, 1978, 1979

Group

• Museum of Modern Art, Paris, 1974 • "America 1976", U.S. Department of the Interior, 1976

• "The Great American Foot", Museum of Contemporary Crafts, Chicago, 1978

• Hunt Institute, Carnegie-Mellon University, 1979

Represented by Andrew Crispo Gallery, New York City

JOSEPH RAFFAEL

Born: Brooklyn, New York, 1933

Education: Cooper Union, Yale University

Current Residence: San Geronimo, California

Selected Exhibitions:

Solo

● University of California, Berkeley, 1973 ● University Art Gallery, Las Vegas, Nevada, 1975

● Museum of Fine Arts, St. Petersberg, Florida, 1977 ● San Francisco Museum of Modern Art (and tour
to Des Moines Art Center, Joslyn Art Museum, Newport Harbor Art Museum and Denver Art Museum), 1978-1979

● Columbus Museum of Arts and Sciences, Columbus, Georgia (and tour to Mint Museum,
Birmingham Art Museum and Jackson State College Gallery), 1980

Group

● "Things Seen", Wichita Art Museum, Kansas (and tour to ten additional cities), 1978-1979

● "Realists", Sheldon Memorial Art Gallery, University of Nebraska, 1978

● "America 1976", U.S. Department of the Interior, 1976

Represented by Nancy Hoffman Gallery, New York City

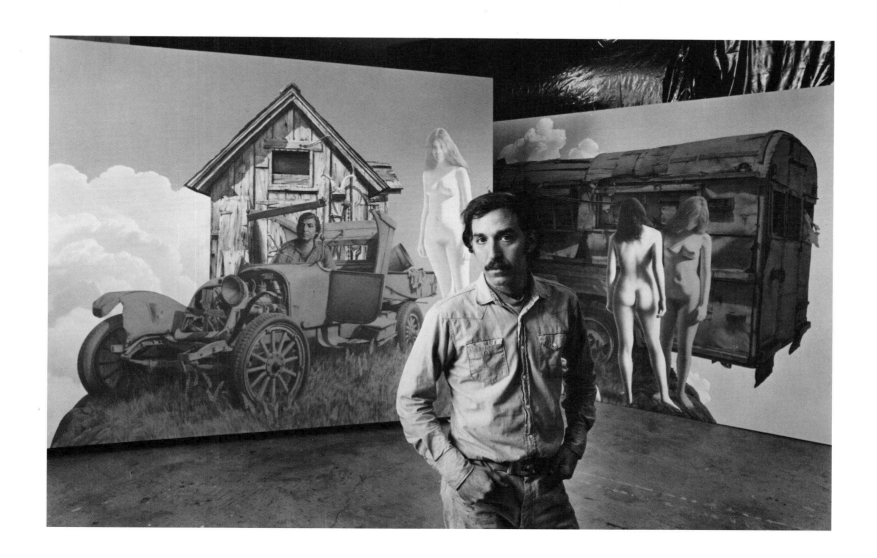

PAUL SARKISIAN

Born: Chicago, Illinois, 1928

Education: School of the Art Institute of Chicago, Otis Art Institute, Mexico City College

Current Residence: Santa Fe, New Mexico

Selected Exhibitions:

Solo

● Pasadena Art Museum, 1968 ● Corcoran Gallery of Art, 1969

● Santa Barbara Museum of Art, 1970 ● Museum of Contemporary Art, Chicago, 1972

● Museum of Contemporary Arts, Houston, 1977 ● Nancy Hoffman Gallery, New York City, 1978 ● The Arts Club, Chicago, 1979

Group

● "Painting and Sculpture Today", Indianapolis Museum of Art, 1976 ● "The Modern Era", National Collection of Fine Arts, 1977

● "Illusions of Reality", Australian National Gallery (and tour throughout Australia), 1977-1978

● "American Art Since 1950", Santa Barbara Museum of Art, 1980

Represented by Nancy Hoffman Gallery, New York City

BEN SCHONZEIT

Born: Brooklyn, New York, 1942

Education: Cooper Union

Current Residence: New York City

Selected Exhibitions:

Solo

• Nancy Hoffman Gallery, New York City, 1973, 1975, 1976, 1978, 1979, 1980

• De Gestlo Gallery, Cologne, 1979 • De Gestlo Gallery, Hamburg, 1971, 1975, 1976, 1978

Group

• "America 1976", U.S. Department of the Interior, 1976 • "The Chosen Object", Joslyn Museum, Omaha, Nebraska, 1977

• "A Century of Master Drawings", Creighton University, Omaha, Nebraska, 1978

• "Things Seen", Sheldon Memorial Art Gallery, University of Nebraska, 1978-1979

Represented by Nancy Hoffman Gallery, New York City

JAMES VALERIO

Born: Chicago, Illinois, 1938

Education: Art Institute of Chicago, Seymour Rosofsky

Current Residence: Ithaca, New York

Selected Exhibitions:

Solo

• Gerard John Hayes Gallery, Los Angeles, California, 1971, 1972 • Tucson Art Center, Tucson, Arizona, 1973
• Michael Walls Gallery, New York City, 1974 • John Berggruen Gallery, San Francisco, California, 1977

Group

• "Imagination", Los Angeles Institute of Contemporary Art, 1976
• "Painting and Sculpture in California: The Modern Era", San Francisco Museum of Modern Art, 1977
• "The Big Still Life", Allan Frumkin Gallery, New York City, 1979

Represented by Allan Frumkin Gallery, New York City

Deluca's Dining Car, Pittsfield, Mass. (1980)

Honest John's (1976)

Stinson Beach Cookout (1978)

Stucco Wall (1977)

Anemones (1980)

Green Table (1979)

Study for "G Series-News 2" (1980)

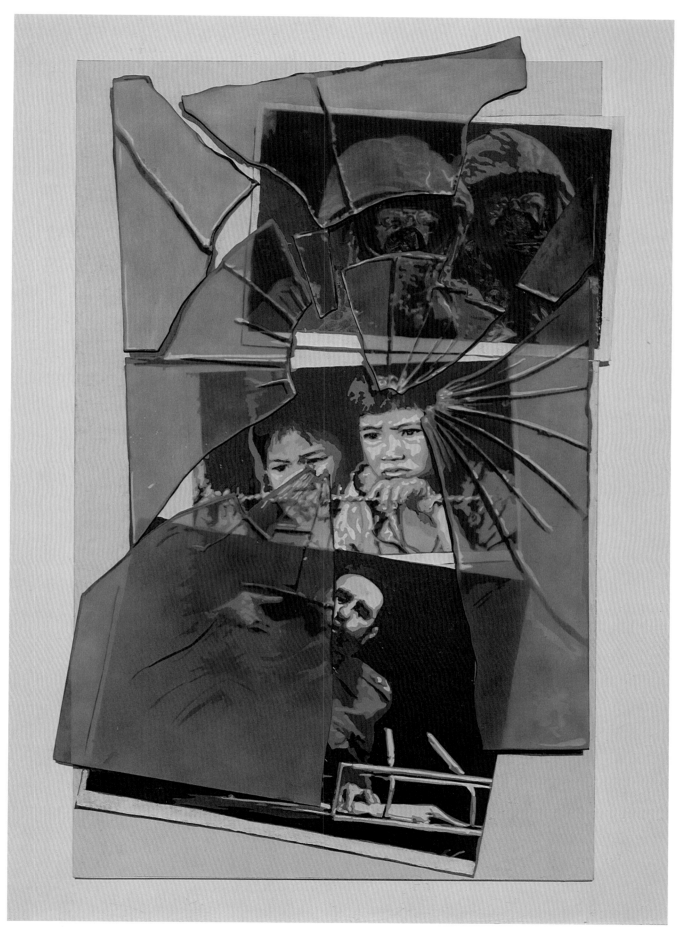

G Series-News 2 (1980)

Cold Beer (1980)

Rat (1978)

Untitled (1976)

Silverware V for S (1977)

Qualicraft Shoes (1975)

Central Savings (1975)

Still Life with Mustard (1980)

Pee Wee's Diner, Warnerville, New York (1977)

Beacon Street (1975)

View North From the Empire State Building (1980)

Everything Must Be Sold! (1975)

Mirrored Dressing Room (1977)

Broome Street Window II – '76 (1976)

Black Parrot Tulip – '78 (1978)

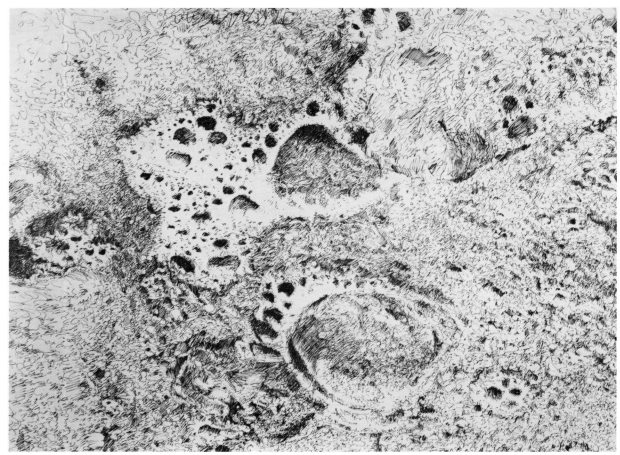

Scottish Bubbles (1975)

Kona II (1975)

Untitled (Milorganite) (1979)

Untitled #5 (1978)

The Music Room #3 (1977)

Short Stuff (1978)

Still Life (1979)

Gail (1977)

(Bold face numbers indicate artist photos and biographies. Light face numbers indicate illustrations of paintings and drawings.)

Lenders to the Exhibition

Allan Stone Gallery, New York
Allen Frumkin Gallery, New York
Stephen S. Alpert, Wayland,
 Massachusetts
Andrew Crispo Gallery, New York
Brooke Alexander, Inc., New York
Charles Campbell Gallery,
 San Francisco
Robert Cottingham, Newtown,
 Connecticut
J. & R. Davidson, Boston
Fischbach Gallery, New York
Harcus Krakow Gallery, Boston

Hirschl & Adler Galleries, Inc.,
 New York
The Sydney and Frances Lewis
 Foundation, Richmond
Marlborough Gallery, Inc.,
 New York
Memorial Art Gallery of the
 University of Rochester
Robert Miller Gallery, New York
Nancy Hoffman Gallery, New York
Nelson Gallery-Atkins Museum
George Nick, Boston
O. K. Harris Works of Art, New York

The Herbert W. Plimpton Collection,
 on extended loan to the Rose Art
 Museum, Brandeis University
The Pollock Family, Waltham,
 Massachusetts
Stephen Posen, New York
Private Collection, Boston
Robert Schoelkopf Gallery, New York
Joseph Shein, Philadelphia
Tibor de Nagy Gallery, New York
The Toledo Museum of Art
Virginia Museum of Fine Arts
The Williams Companies of Tulsa

Photo Credits for Realism/Photo-Realism

John Arthur
(portrait of Jack Beal) – 20
(portrait of Robert Bechtle) – 74
(portrait of William Beckman) – 21
(portrait of Richard Estes) – 79
(portrait of Janet Fish) – 23
(portrait of Richard Haas) – 81
(portrait of Alfred Leslie) – 26
(portrait of John Moore) – 27
(portrait of Philip Pearlstein) – 29
Posen, UNTITLED – 58

Bob Brooks
(portrait of John Button) – 22
(portrait of Jane Freilicher) – 24

Bevan Davies
Brady, ANEMONES – 92
Eddy, UNTITLED – 98
Raffael, SCOTTISH BUBBLES – 110
Sarkisian, UNTITLED – 112

Dayton Art Institute
Fairfield Porter, self portrait – 30

D. James Dee
Baeder, DELUCCA'S DINING CAR – 88
Baeder, HONEST JOHN'S – 89
Bechtle, STINSON BEACH COOKOUT – 90
Clarke, study for G SERIES – NEWS 2 – 94
Clarke, G SERIES – NEWS 2 – 95

Goings, STILL LIFE WITH MUSTARD – 102
Mendenhall, EVERYTHING MUST
 BE SOLD! – 106

Eeva – Inkeri
Bailey, HEAD OF A GIRL – 34
Fish, SPOONS AND CARNATIONS – 42
Pearlstein, TWO FEMALE MODELS,
 SEATED AND RECLINING ON
 INDIAN RUG – 54
(portrait of Wayne Thiebaud; self-portrait
painting; collection of Mr. and Mrs. E. A.
Bergman, Chicago) – 32

Bill Foote
(portrait of Paul Sarkisian) – 85

Helga Photo Studio
Porter, SUN AND SEA – 56

Ada Katz
(portrait of Alex Katz) – 25

Wayne O. Lemmon
Cottingham, RAT – 97
Beal, PORTRAIT OF JOHN ARTHUR – 36
Cottingham, COLD BEER – 96
Estes, QUALICRAFT SHOES – 100
Goings, PEE WEE'S DINER – 103
Haas, BEACON STREET – 104
Katz, VINCENT IN CANOE – 46
Nick, PIAZZA DEL POPOLO – 52

Valerio, GAIL – 117
Welliver, PROSPECT BROOK – 63

Nancy K. Lloyd
(portrait of Ralph Goings) – 80

Ralph Snow MacKenzie
(portrait of George Nick) – 28

Bob McCormack
Thiebaud, STILL LIFE
 WITH BOWL – 60

Muldoon Studios, Waltham, Mass.
Bailey, MANFRONI STILL LIFE – 35
Sarkisian, UNTITLED #5 – 113

Edward Peterson
Button, 23RD STREET
 HIGH NOON – 40
Freilicher, PEONY – 44
Moore, UNTITLED – 50

Eric Pollitzer
Leslie, REBECCA WERNER – 48

Quiriconi–Tropea Photographers
Valerio, STILL LIFE – 116

Jerry L. Thompson
(portrait of William Bailey) – 19

Abby Zonies
(portrait of Neil Welliver) – 33